Guide To Kids ADHD

:

A Guide To Understanding And Supporting Kids With ADHD

Introduction

Welcome to "A Guide to Understanding and Supporting Kids with ADHD." In the journey of parenting or working with children with ADHD, understanding and support are paramount. This book aims to provide insights, strategies, and practical tips for caregivers, educators, and anyone involved in the lives of children with Attention Deficit Hyperactivity Disorder (ADHD). By fostering a supportive environment and employing effective techniques, we can empower children with ADHD to thrive and reach their full potential.

A Guide to Understanding and Supporting Kids with ADHD." This book is a comprehensive resource designed to provide parents, caregivers, educators, and healthcare professionals with valuable insights, practical strategies, and evidence-based approaches for effectively supporting children with Attention-Deficit/Hyperactivity Disorder (ADHD).

ADHD is a neurodevelopmental disorder that affects millions of children worldwide, impacting their attention, impulse control, and behavior. Children with ADHD often face challenges in various aspects of their lives, including academics, social interactions, and emotional regulation. Understanding ADHD and its impact on children is the first step toward providing them with the support and resources they need to thrive.

In this guide, we will explore the multifaceted nature of ADHD, examining its causes, symptoms, diagnosis, and the impact it has on children and families. We will delve into practical strategies for creating supportive environments, establishing routines, and fostering positive relationships. Additionally, we will discuss effective communication techniques, collaboration with schools, and the importance of individualized education plans (IEPs) and 504 plans.

Throughout the book, we will emphasize the importance of promoting self-regulation skills, incorporating mindfulness and relaxation techniques, and exploring alternative treatments and therapies. We will also address the challenges of managing impulsivity, addressing oppositional behaviors, and coping with frustration and rejection.

As advocates for children with ADHD, it is our responsibility to ensure that they receive the understanding, support, and accommodations they need to reach their full potential. By equipping ourselves with knowledge, empathy, and practical tools, we can empower children with ADHD to navigate life's challenges with confidence and resilience.

Whether you are a parent seeking guidance, an educator striving to create inclusive classrooms, or a healthcare professional supporting children with ADHD, this guide is intended to be a valuable resource on your journey toward understanding and supporting kids with ADHD.

Together, let us embark on this journey of compassion, learning, and advocacy for the well-being of children with ADHD.

Table Of Contents

Chapter 1: Understanding ADHD

- **1.1 What is ADHD in Children?**
- **1.2 Causes and Risk Factors**
- **1.3 Recognizing Symptoms and Diagnosis**
- **1.4 The Impact of ADHD on Children and Families**

1.1 What is ADHD?

ADHD, or Attention Deficit Hyperactivity Disorder, is a neurodevelopmental disorder commonly diagnosed in children. It is characterized by persistent patterns of inattention, impulsivity, and hyperactivity that interfere with functioning or development.

Here are some key aspects of ADHD in kids:

Inattention: Children with ADHD often have difficulty sustaining attention on tasks or activities, especially those that require focused mental effort. They may seem forgetful, easily distracted, and have trouble organizing tasks or following instructions.

Hyperactivity: Hyperactivity manifests as excessive fidgeting, restlessness, and difficulty staying seated, particularly in situations where it's expected. Children with ADHD may appear to be constantly on the go and have trouble engaging in quiet activities.

Impulsivity: Impulsivity refers to acting without thinking about consequences. Children with ADHD may blurt out answers, interrupt others, and have difficulty waiting their turn in conversations or activities. They may also have trouble controlling emotional reactions.

Onset and Persistence: Symptoms of ADHD typically appear in early childhood, often before the age of 12, and can persist into adolescence and adulthood. While some children may outgrow certain symptoms as they mature, others may continue to experience challenges associated with ADHD throughout their lives.

Impact on Daily Functioning: ADHD can significantly impact various aspects of a child's life, including academic performance, social relationships, and behavior at home and school. It can affect their ability to succeed academically, follow rules, and interact with peers.

Co-occurring Conditions: Children with ADHD may also experience co-occurring conditions such as learning disabilities, anxiety disorders, depression, and oppositional defiant disorder (ODD). These conditions can further complicate the management and treatment of ADHD symptoms.

Individual Differences: It's important to recognize that ADHD presents differently in each child. Some children may primarily exhibit symptoms of inattention, while others may display more prominent hyperactivity and impulsivity. The severity of symptoms can also vary widely among children with ADHD.

Diagnosis and Treatment: Diagnosis of ADHD involves a comprehensive evaluation by healthcare professionals, including pediatricians, psychologists, and psychiatrists. Treatment options may include behavioral therapy, medication, educational interventions, and parent training programs, tailored to meet the specific needs of the child.

Understanding ADHD in children involves recognizing the complex interplay of biological, environmental, and developmental factors that contribute to the disorder. With early identification, appropriate interventions, and ongoing support, children with ADHD can learn to manage their symptoms and thrive in various aspects of their lives.

1.2 Causes and Risk Factors

The exact causes of Attention Deficit Hyperactivity Disorder (ADHD) are not fully understood, but research suggests that a combination of genetic, environmental, and neurological factors contribute to its development. Here are some key factors associated with the causes and risk factors of ADHD:

Genetic Factors: Genetics play a significant role in the development of ADHD. Studies have shown that ADHD tends to run in families, indicating a strong genetic component. Children with a family history of ADHD are at a higher risk of developing the disorder themselves.

Neurological Differences: Research has identified differences in brain structure and function in individuals with ADHD, particularly in areas of the brain that regulate attention, impulse control, and executive functions. Neurotransmitters such as dopamine and norepinephrine, which play a role in attention and behavior regulation, may also be involved.

Prenatal and Perinatal Factors: Certain prenatal and perinatal factors have been linked to an increased risk of ADHD. These include maternal smoking, alcohol or substance abuse during pregnancy, premature birth, low birth weight, and exposure to environmental toxins.

Brain Injury or Trauma: Traumatic brain injury or other types of brain damage can increase the likelihood of developing ADHD symptoms. Injury to areas of the brain responsible for attention, impulse control, and executive functions can disrupt normal neurological development and contribute to ADHD symptoms.

Environmental Factors: Environmental influences, such as exposure to lead or other toxins, prenatal maternal stress, early childhood adversity, and disrupted family environments, may also contribute to the development of

ADHD. While these factors alone may not cause ADHD, they can interact with genetic predispositions and neurological vulnerabilities to increase the risk.

Parenting and Family Dynamics: While parenting style itself does not cause ADHD, certain parenting practices and family dynamics can exacerbate or mitigate ADHD symptoms. Inconsistent discipline, lack of structure, and high levels of stress within the family environment may contribute to behavioral difficulties in children with ADHD.

Co-occurring Conditions: ADHD often co-occurs with other mental health disorders, such as anxiety disorders, depression, learning disabilities, and conduct disorders. The presence of these co-occurring conditions can complicate the diagnosis and treatment of ADHD and may contribute to the severity of symptoms.

It's important to recognize that ADHD is a complex and multifaceted disorder influenced by a variety of factors. While the exact causes may vary from one individual to another, understanding the interplay of genetic, neurological, environmental, and developmental factors is crucial for effective diagnosis, treatment, and support for individuals with ADHD. Early identification and intervention can help mitigate the impact of ADHD symptoms and improve long-term outcomes for affected individuals.

1.3 Recognizing Symptoms and Diagnosis

Recognizing symptoms of ADHD and obtaining an accurate diagnosis are essential steps in providing appropriate support and interventions for children who may be affected by the disorder. ADHD presents with a range of symptoms that can manifest differently in each child. Here are some key aspects to consider when recognizing symptoms and seeking a diagnosis:

Symptoms of Inattention:

- Difficulty paying attention to details and making careless mistakes in schoolwork or other activities.

- Trouble staying focused on tasks, particularly those that require sustained mental effort.

- Difficulty organizing tasks and activities.

- Frequently losing necessary items like school supplies or toys.

- Easily distracted by external stimuli.

- Forgetfulness in daily activities.

Symptoms of Hyperactivity:

- Constantly fidgeting or squirming, particularly in situations where it is inappropriate.

- Difficulty remaining seated in situations where staying seated is expected, such as in the classroom or during meals.

- Often running or climbing excessively in inappropriate situations.

- Difficulty engaging in leisure activities quietly.

- Talks excessively or blurts out answers before questions are complete.

Symptoms of Impulsivity:

- Acting without thinking about consequences.

- Interrupting or intruding on others' conversations or activities.

- Difficulty waiting for one's turn in activities or conversations.

- Difficulty following rules and instructions, especially in structured environments like school.

Duration and Severity:

- Symptoms of ADHD must persist for at least six months and be present in multiple settings, such as home, school, and social environments.

- The severity of symptoms and the degree to which they interfere with daily functioning can vary among children.

Age of Onset:

- Symptoms of ADHD typically appear in early childhood, often before the age of 12, although they may become more noticeable as academic and social demands increase.

Differential Diagnosis:

- Other medical, developmental, or behavioral conditions can mimic symptoms of ADHD, so it's important to consider alternative explanations and rule out other potential causes before making a diagnosis.

Multidisciplinary Evaluation:

- Diagnosis of ADHD involves a comprehensive evaluation by healthcare professionals, including pediatricians, child psychologists, psychiatrists, and other specialists.

- The evaluation may include a thorough medical history, observation of the child's behavior in different settings, standardized rating scales completed by parents, teachers, and caregivers, as well as assessments of cognitive and academic functioning.

Cultural Considerations:

- Recognizing that cultural factors may influence the expression and interpretation of ADHD symptoms is important in the diagnostic process.

Collaboration with Parents and Educators:

- Parents and educators play a crucial role in providing information about the child's behavior and functioning in various settings, which can help inform the diagnostic process.

Obtaining a comprehensive understanding of the child's symptoms, functioning, and developmental history is key to making an accurate diagnosis of ADHD. Early identification and intervention can help children with ADHD receive the support and resources they need to succeed academically, socially, and emotionally.

1.4 The Impact of ADHD on Children and Families

The impact of Attention Deficit Hyperactivity Disorder (ADHD) on children and families can be profound and far-reaching, affecting various aspects of daily life and functioning. Understanding these impacts is crucial for providing appropriate support and interventions. Here are some key areas where ADHD can have an impact:

Academic Performance: Children with ADHD may struggle with academic tasks that require sustained attention, organization, and self-control. They may have difficulty completing homework assignments, following classroom instructions, and staying focused during lectures or independent study. Academic achievement may be compromised, leading to frustration, low self-esteem, and feelings of inadequacy.

Social Relationships: ADHD can affect a child's ability to develop and maintain positive social relationships with peers and family members. Impulsivity, hyperactivity, and difficulty regulating emotions may lead to social difficulties, such as interrupting others, engaging in risky behaviors, or experiencing conflicts with peers. Children with ADHD may struggle with social cues, empathy, and perspective-taking, making it challenging to navigate social interactions effectively.

Emotional Regulation: Children with ADHD may experience heightened emotional reactivity and difficulty regulating their emotions. They may be more prone to mood swings, frustration, anger outbursts, and emotional dysregulation in response to stressors or challenges. Emotional dysregulation can impact family dynamics and contribute to conflicts and tensions within the household.

Behavioral Challenges: Impulsivity, hyperactivity, and inattention can manifest as behavioral challenges both at home and in school. Children with ADHD may engage in disruptive behaviors, such as talking out of turn, blurting out answers, or engaging in physical aggression. These behaviors can lead to disciplinary issues, strained relationships with authority figures, and negative peer interactions.

Family Stress and Dysfunction: Managing the challenges associated with ADHD can place significant stress on families, leading to feelings of frustration, guilt, and exhaustion among parents and caregivers. Sibling relationships may be affected as parents devote additional time and attention to managing the needs of the child with ADHD. Family routines and dynamics may be disrupted, leading to increased conflict and tension within the household.

Parental Mental Health: Parents of children with ADHD may experience higher levels of stress, anxiety, and depression compared to parents of neurotypical children. Balancing the demands of caregiving, advocating for their child's needs, and addressing behavioral challenges can take a toll on parental well-being and mental health.

Financial Strain: The financial costs associated with managing ADHD, including medical expenses, therapy sessions, educational support, and specialized interventions, can place a strain on families' financial resources.

Long-Term Outcomes: Untreated or inadequately managed ADHD can have long-term implications for children's academic and occupational outcomes, as well as their overall quality of life into adulthood.

Recognizing the impact of ADHD on children and families underscores the importance of early identification, comprehensive assessment, and access to evidence-based interventions and support services. By addressing the multifaceted needs of children with ADHD and their families, it is possible to promote positive outcomes and enhance overall well-being.

Chapter 2: Strategies for Managing ADHD

- **2.1 Creating a Supportive Environment**
- **2.2 Establishing Routines and Structure**
- **2.3 Effective Communication Techniques**
- **2.4 Encouraging Self-Regulation Skills**
- **2.5 Incorporating Mindfulness and Relaxation Techniques**

2.1 Creating a Supportive Environment

Creating a supportive environment is essential for children with ADHD to thrive and succeed in various aspects of their lives. A supportive environment encompasses home, school, and community settings where children feel understood, accepted, and empowered to reach their full potential. Here are some strategies for creating a supportive environment for children with ADHD:

Promote Understanding and Awareness: Educate family members, teachers, peers, and community members about ADHD, including its symptoms, challenges, and strengths. Foster empathy and dispel misconceptions about ADHD to promote acceptance and understanding of the unique needs of children with the disorder.

Establish Clear and Consistent Expectations: Set clear and age-appropriate expectations for behavior, routines, and academic tasks at home and in school. Use visual aids, schedules, and reminders to help children with ADHD understand expectations and transitions.

Provide Structure and Predictability: Establish consistent routines and daily schedules to help children with ADHD feel secure and organized. Break tasks and activities into manageable steps, providing clear instructions and support as needed. Minimize transitions and unexpected changes whenever possible, providing advance notice and preparation when changes are unavoidable.

Create a Positive and Nurturing Environment: Provide praise, encouragement, and positive reinforcement to recognize children's efforts and achievements. Focus on strengths and areas of interest, fostering a sense of competence and self-confidence. Foster a nurturing and supportive relationship between caregivers and children, emphasizing unconditional love and acceptance.

Teach and Reinforce Self-Regulation Skills: Teach children with ADHD strategies for self-regulation, including mindfulness, deep breathing exercises, and relaxation techniques. Help children recognize and express their emotions in constructive ways, providing tools and coping strategies for managing frustration, anxiety, and impulsivity.

Encourage Independence and Self-Advocacy: Empower children with ADHD to take ownership of their learning, behavior, and self-care routines. Teach self-advocacy skills, such as asking for help, seeking clarification, and expressing needs and preferences to teachers, peers, and caregivers.

Provide Opportunities for Physical Activity and Movement: Incorporate regular opportunities for physical activity and movement breaks throughout the day to help children with ADHD release excess energy and improve focus and concentration. Encourage participation in sports, recreational activities, and outdoor play to promote physical health and well-being.

Establish Effective Communication Channels: Maintain open and collaborative communication between parents, teachers, and other caregivers to share insights, concerns, and strategies for supporting children with ADHD. Encourage children to communicate their needs, preferences, and challenges openly and respectfully, fostering a sense of agency and partnership in problem-solving.

Creating a supportive environment for children with ADHD requires collaboration, patience, and flexibility among caregivers, educators, and community members. By implementing these strategies and fostering a culture of understanding and acceptance, we can empower children with ADHD to thrive and succeed in all aspects of their lives.

<u>2.2 Establishing Routines and Structure</u>

Establishing routines and structure is crucial for children with ADHD to feel grounded, organized, and supported in their daily lives. Consistent routines provide predictability, help manage transitions, and promote independence and self-regulation. Here are some strategies for establishing effective routines and structure for children with ADHD:

Create a Daily Schedule: Develop a structured daily schedule that includes consistent wake-up times, meal times, bedtime routines, and designated times for homework, chores, and leisure activities. Display the schedule visually using charts, calendars, or electronic devices to help children understand and follow the routine.

Break Tasks into Manageable Steps: Break down larger tasks or activities into smaller, manageable steps to prevent overwhelm and facilitate task completion. Use visual cues, checklists, or written instructions to guide children through each step of the process and monitor progress.

Set Clear Expectations: Clearly communicate expectations for behavior, responsibilities, and academic tasks within the home and school environments. Use positive language to reinforce desired behaviors and provide specific feedback and praise for compliance with expectations.

Use Visual Supports: Visual supports, such as visual schedules, timers, and reminders, can help children with ADHD stay organized, manage time effectively, and transition between activities smoothly. Visual cues provide concrete and tangible guidance, reducing reliance on verbal instructions and minimizing misunderstandings.

Establish Consistent Rules and Consequences: Establish consistent rules and consequences for behavior, emphasizing logical and age-appropriate consequences for both positive and negative behaviors. Be consistent in enforcing rules and follow through with consequences to promote accountability and reinforce expectations.

Minimize Distractions: Create a supportive environment free from distractions that can interfere with attention and focus. Designate a quiet and clutter-free study area for homework and academic tasks, and limit access to electronic devices and other potential distractions during designated study times.

Encourage Time Management Skills: Teach children with ADHD time management skills, such as prioritizing tasks, estimating time accurately, and using timers or alarms to help them stay on track. Model effective time management strategies and provide opportunities for practice and reinforcement.

Incorporate Regular Breaks and Movement: Incorporate regular breaks and movement opportunities throughout the day to help children with ADHD release excess energy, improve focus and concentration, and reduce feelings of restlessness or impulsivity. Encourage physical activities, sensory breaks, or brief movement breaks between tasks or during transitions.

Flexibility and Adaptability: While routines provide structure and predictability, it's important to remain flexible and adaptable to accommodate changes, unexpected events, and individual needs. Allow for adjustments to routines as needed and involve children in decision-making processes to promote ownership and engagement.

Monitor and Adjust: Monitor the effectiveness of routines and structure regularly, soliciting feedback from children, caregivers, and educators to identify areas for improvement or modification. Adjust routines and strategies based on individual needs and preferences to optimize support and promote success.

By establishing consistent routines and structure, caregivers and educators can create a supportive environment that fosters independence, self-regulation, and success for children with ADHD. These strategies promote predictability, organization, and stability, empowering children to navigate daily challenges with confidence and resilience.

2.3   Effective   Communication Techniques

Effective communication techniques are essential for fostering understanding, collaboration, and support for children with ADHD. Clear and positive communication strategies help build trust, reinforce positive behaviors, and address challenges proactively. Here are some effective communication techniques for interacting with children with ADHD:

Use Clear and Concise Language: Use simple, direct language to convey instructions, expectations, and information to children with ADHD. Break down complex ideas or tasks into smaller, more manageable components to facilitate understanding and comprehension.

Maintain Eye Contact and Nonverbal Cues: Establish eye contact and use appropriate facial expressions, gestures, and body language to convey warmth, attentiveness, and engagement. Nonverbal cues can help reinforce verbal messages and enhance communication effectiveness.

Provide Positive Feedback and Encouragement: Offer specific and genuine praise for desirable behaviors, efforts, and achievements to reinforce positive behavior and motivate continued progress. Focus on strengths and accomplishments, highlighting areas of improvement and growth.

Active Listening: Practice active listening by giving full attention to the child, maintaining eye contact, and providing verbal and nonverbal cues that demonstrate understanding and empathy. Validate the child's feelings, thoughts, and experiences, acknowledging their perspective and feelings without judgment.

Encourage Two-Way Communication: Foster open and reciprocal communication by encouraging children to express their thoughts, feelings, and concerns freely. Create a safe and supportive environment where children feel comfortable sharing their experiences and perspectives without fear of criticism or rejection.

Clarify Expectations and Instructions: Clearly articulate expectations, instructions, and guidelines using simple language and visual supports to help children understand and follow directions effectively. Break down tasks into smaller steps and provide concrete examples or demonstrations to illustrate expectations.

Offer Choices and Empowerment: Provide opportunities for children to make choices and exercise autonomy within appropriate boundaries. Offer alternatives and options whenever possible, allowing children to participate in decision-making processes and take ownership of their actions and outcomes.

Use Positive Reinforcement and Behavior Management Techniques: Implement positive reinforcement strategies, such as praise, rewards, and incentives, to encourage desired behaviors and motivate children to achieve goals. Use behavior management techniques, such as token systems or behavior charts, to track progress and reinforce positive behaviors consistently.

Be Patient and Flexible: Practice patience and flexibility when communicating with children with ADHD, recognizing that they may require additional time, support, and repetition to understand and process information effectively. Be willing to adapt communication strategies and approaches based on individual needs and preferences.

Seek Collaborative Solutions: Involve children in problem-solving and decision-making processes, soliciting their input and ideas for finding solutions to challenges or conflicts. Collaborate with parents, educators, and other caregivers to develop consistent communication strategies and support plans that promote the child's well-being and success.

By employing effective communication techniques, caregivers, educators, and other support providers can build positive relationships, enhance self-esteem, and empower children with ADHD to navigate challenges and thrive in various settings. Open, empathetic, and respectful communication lays the foundation for meaningful connections and positive outcomes for children with ADHD.

<u>2.4   Encouraging   Self-Regulation Skills</u>

Encouraging self-regulation skills is essential for children with ADHD to manage their emotions, behavior, and attention effectively. Self-regulation skills enable children to understand and control their impulses, emotions, and reactions in various situations, promoting adaptive coping strategies and positive social interactions. Here are some strategies for encouraging self-regulation skills in children with ADHD:

Model Self-Regulation Behaviors: Serve as a positive role model by demonstrating self-regulation behaviors, such as staying calm in stressful situations, using coping strategies to manage emotions, and practicing patience and perseverance when facing challenges. Children learn by observing and imitating adult behaviors, so modeling self-regulation skills is crucial.

Teach Emotional Awareness: Help children develop awareness of their emotions by labeling and identifying different feelings, such as happiness, sadness, anger, and frustration. Encourage children to express their emotions verbally and nonverbally, validating their feelings and experiences without judgment.

Practice Mindfulness and Relaxation Techniques: Introduce mindfulness and relaxation techniques, such as deep breathing exercises, progressive muscle relaxation, and guided imagery, to help children manage stress, anxiety, and impulsivity. Teach children to focus their attention on the present moment and cultivate a sense of calm and inner peace.

Provide Sensory Regulation Strategies: Recognize the sensory needs of children with ADHD and provide sensory regulation strategies to help them maintain optimal arousal levels and focus. Offer sensory tools and activities, such as fidget toys, sensory bins, and sensory breaks, to promote self-regulation and sensory integration.

Set Realistic Goals and Expectations: Establish realistic and achievable goals for self-regulation, focusing on incremental progress and improvement over time. Break down larger goals into smaller, manageable steps, providing children with a clear roadmap for success and celebrating their accomplishments along the way.

Encourage Problem-Solving Skills: Teach children problem-solving skills and strategies for resolving conflicts, making decisions, and finding solutions to challenges independently. Encourage critical thinking, creativity, and flexibility in approaching problems, empowering children to take initiative and exercise autonomy.

Implement Behavior Management Techniques: Implement behavior management techniques, such as positive reinforcement, token systems, and behavior contracts, to promote self-regulation and reinforce desired behaviors. Provide immediate feedback and praise for self-regulatory efforts, highlighting progress and positive changes.

Establish Consistent Routines and Structure: Create a structured and predictable environment with consistent routines, rules, and expectations to support self-regulation and minimize impulsivity. Help children anticipate and prepare for transitions and changes by providing advance notice and visual cues.

Teach Self-monitoring Skills: Teach children to monitor and evaluate their own behavior, attention, and emotions using self-monitoring tools, such as behavior charts, checklists, and self-assessment scales. Encourage children to reflect on their strengths, challenges, and areas for improvement, fostering self-awareness and self-reflection.

Provide Positive Reinforcement and Encouragement: Offer positive reinforcement, encouragement, and praise for efforts and progress in developing self-regulation skills.

Acknowledge children's successes and perseverance in managing their behavior and emotions, reinforcing their intrinsic motivation and self-confidence.

By incorporating these strategies into daily routines and interactions, caregivers, educators, and other support providers can help children with ADHD develop and strengthen their self-regulation skills, promoting resilience, autonomy, and overall well-being. Encouraging self-regulation empowers children to navigate challenges effectively and achieve their full potential in various aspects of their lives.

2.5 Incorporating Mindfulness and Relaxation Techniques

Incorporating mindfulness and relaxation techniques can be highly beneficial for children with ADHD, helping them to reduce stress, improve focus, and regulate emotions effectively. Here are some mindfulness and relaxation techniques that can be adapted for children with ADHD:

Deep Breathing Exercises: Teach children simple deep breathing exercises to help them calm their minds and bodies. Encourage them to take slow, deep breaths in through their nose, hold for a few seconds, and then exhale slowly through their mouth. Practice this technique during moments of stress or agitation.

Mindful Breathing: Guide children to focus their attention on their breath, noticing the sensation of air entering and leaving their nostrils or the rise and fall of their chest and abdomen. Encourage them to bring their attention back to their breath whenever their mind wanders.

Body Scan Meditation: Lead children through a body scan meditation, where they focus their attention on different parts of their body, starting from their toes and gradually moving up to their head. Encourage them to notice any sensations, tension, or discomfort in each body part and practice letting go of tension with each exhale.

Guided Imagery: Use guided imagery exercises to help children visualize calming and peaceful scenes, such as a quiet beach, a serene forest, or a cozy cabin in the mountains. Encourage them to engage their senses and imagine themselves in a safe and tranquil environment.

Progressive Muscle Relaxation: Teach children progressive muscle relaxation techniques by guiding them to tense and relax different muscle groups in their body systematically. Start with their toes and work their way up to their shoulders, instructing them to tense each muscle group for a few seconds before releasing and relaxing.

Mindful Movement: Incorporate mindful movement practices, such as yoga, tai chi, or qigong, into children's daily routines. Encourage them to focus on their breath and body sensations as they move through gentle and flowing movements, promoting relaxation, flexibility, and body awareness.

Mindful Eating: Practice mindful eating by encouraging children to pay attention to the taste, texture, and smell of their food without judgment or distraction. Encourage them to eat slowly, savoring each bite and noticing the sensations of hunger and fullness.

Nature Walks: Take children on nature walks or outdoor excursions to connect with the natural world and engage their senses. Encourage them to notice the sights, sounds, and smells of their surroundings, fostering a sense of curiosity, wonder, and mindfulness.

Breathing Buddies: Invite children to choose a small stuffed animal or object to serve as their "breathing buddy." Encourage them to place the buddy on their belly and observe how it rises and falls with each breath, promoting awareness of their breathing and grounding in the present moment.

Mindful Listening: Practice mindful listening activities by inviting children to close their eyes and focus their attention on different sounds in their environment, such as birds chirping, leaves rustling, or cars passing by. Encourage them to notice each sound without judgment or interpretation.

By incorporating mindfulness and relaxation techniques into children's daily routines and activities, caregivers, educators, and other support providers can help children with ADHD cultivate greater self-awareness, emotional regulation, and resilience. These practices promote a sense of calm, balance, and well-being, empowering children to navigate challenges and thrive in various aspects of their lives.

Chapter 3: Educational Support

- **3.1 Collaboration with Teachers and School Staff**
- **3.2 Individualized Education Plans (IEPs) and 504 Plans**
- **3.3 Classroom Accommodations and Modifications**
- **3.4 Strategies for Homework and Study Skills**

3.1 Collaboration with Teachers and School Staff

Collaboration with teachers and school staff is essential for supporting children with ADHD in the educational setting and promoting their academic success, social development, and overall well-being. Effective communication, collaboration, and partnership between parents, caregivers, educators, and school personnel are key to creating a supportive and inclusive environment for children with ADHD. Here are some strategies for fostering collaboration with teachers and school staff:

Open and Transparent Communication: Establish open lines of communication with your child's teachers and school staff from the outset. Share information about your child's ADHD diagnosis, strengths, challenges, and individualized needs. Keep teachers informed about any changes in medication, therapy, or home routines that may impact your child's behavior or learning.

Attend Parent-Teacher Conferences and Meetings: Participate actively in parent-teacher conferences, Individualized Education Plan (IEP) meetings, and other school meetings to discuss your child's progress, goals, and areas of concern. Listen to the perspectives and insights of teachers and school staff, and collaborate on strategies and interventions to support your child's learning and development.

Share Relevant Information and Resources: Provide teachers and school staff with information and resources about ADHD, evidence-based interventions, and best practices for supporting children with ADHD in the classroom. Offer suggestions for accommodations, modifications, and behavioral strategies that have been effective for your child in the past.

Develop a Collaborative Action Plan: Work together with teachers and school staff to develop a collaborative action plan that outlines specific goals, accommodations, and supports for your child with ADHD. Tailor interventions and strategies to address your child's individual needs, learning style, and preferences.

Implement Classroom Accommodations and Supports: Advocate for classroom accommodations and supports that can help your child with ADHD succeed academically and socially. Examples may include preferential seating, extended time on assignments or tests, breaks during tasks, and access to fidget tools or sensory breaks.

Provide Regular Progress Updates: Keep teachers and school staff informed about your child's progress, achievements, and challenges on a regular basis. Share observations from home about your child's behavior, mood, and well-being, and inquire about any concerns or observations from the school setting.

Collaborate on Behavior Management Strategies: Collaborate with teachers and school staff to develop and implement consistent behavior management strategies that promote positive behavior and self-regulation in the classroom. Establish clear expectations, reinforcement systems, and consequences for behavior, and maintain open communication about behavioral concerns and successes.

Participate in School-Based Interventions and Support Services: Take advantage of school-based interventions and support services, such as counseling, social skills groups, and academic support programs, that can benefit children with ADHD. Collaborate with school personnel to identify appropriate interventions and monitor your child's progress.

Stay Informed About Educational Rights and Resources: Familiarize yourself with your child's educational rights under federal laws such as the Individuals with Disabilities Education Act (IDEA) and Section 504 of the Rehabilitation Act. Advocate for appropriate accommodations, services, and supports to ensure that your child receives a free and appropriate public education (FAPE).

Express Appreciation and Recognition: Show appreciation and recognition for the efforts and dedication of teachers and school staff in supporting your child with ADHD. Acknowledge their commitment to your child's academic and emotional well-being, and express gratitude for their collaboration and partnership.

By fostering a collaborative and supportive relationship with teachers and school staff, parents and caregivers can help create an inclusive and nurturing learning environment where children with ADHD can thrive academically, socially, and emotionally. Effective collaboration enhances communication, understanding, and teamwork, ultimately benefiting the entire school community.

3.2 Individualized Education Plans (IEPs) and 504 Plans

Individualized Education Plans (IEPs) and 504 Plans are legal documents designed to provide supports and accommodations for students with disabilities, including ADHD, in the educational setting. While both plans aim to ensure that students receive the necessary accommodations and services to access their education, there are key differences between them:

Individualized Education Plan (IEP):

- An IEP is a legally binding document developed for students who qualify for special education services under the Individuals with Disabilities Education Act (IDEA).

- To qualify for an IEP, a student must meet the criteria for one or more of the 13 disability categories outlined in IDEA, which includes specific learning disabilities, emotional disturbance, autism, and other health impairments.

- The IEP team, which includes parents, teachers, school administrators, and other relevant professionals, develops an individualized education program tailored to the unique needs of the student.

- The IEP outlines the student's present levels of academic and functional performance, measurable annual goals, special education and related services, accommodations and modifications, and progress monitoring procedures.

- IEPs are comprehensive plans that address all aspects of the student's education, including academic, social, emotional, and behavioral needs.

- IEPs are reviewed and updated annually, with input from all members of the IEP team, to reflect the student's progress and evolving needs.

<u>504 Plan:</u>

- A 504 Plan is a formalized accommodation plan developed under Section 504 of the Rehabilitation Act of 1973, which prohibits discrimination against individuals with disabilities in federally funded programs and activities.

- Unlike an IEP, a 504 Plan does not require that a student qualify for special education services. Instead, it provides accommodations and supports to ensure equal access to education for students with disabilities who do not require specialized instruction.

- A student may qualify for a 504 Plan if they have a physical or mental impairment that substantially limits one or more major life activities, such as learning, reading, concentrating, or interacting with others.

- The 504 Plan outlines specific accommodations, modifications, and supports that the school will provide to address the student's needs and facilitate their participation and progress in the general education curriculum.

- The development and implementation of a 504 Plan typically involve input from parents, teachers, school administrators, and other relevant school personnel.

- 504 Plans are reviewed periodically to assess the effectiveness of accommodations and modifications and make adjustments as needed based on the student's changing needs.

In summary, while both IEPs and 504 Plans aim to provide support and accommodations for students with disabilities, they differ in terms of eligibility criteria, scope of services, and legal requirements. The decision to develop an IEP or a 504 Plan depends on the student's individual needs, eligibility for special education services, and the nature and extent of accommodations and supports required to ensure access to education.

3.3 Classroom Accommodations and Modifications

Classroom accommodations and modifications are essential components of supporting students with ADHD in the educational setting. These accommodations and modifications are designed to address the unique needs and challenges that students with ADHD may experience, helping them access the curriculum, participate effectively in classroom activities, and succeed academically. Here are some examples of classroom accommodations and modifications for students with ADHD:

Seating Arrangements: Provide preferential seating near the front of the classroom or away from distractions to minimize distractions and enhance focus. Allow flexible seating options such as stability balls, standing desks, or fidget cushions to accommodate students' need for movement and sensory input.

Visual Supports: Use visual schedules, calendars, and timers to help students with ADHD understand routines, transitions, and time management. Display visual reminders of classroom rules, expectations, and procedures to reinforce consistency and promote self-regulation.

Structured Routines and Predictability: Establish consistent daily routines and schedules to provide structure and predictability for students with ADHD. Clearly communicate transitions and changes in activities in advance, using visual and verbal cues to prepare students for upcoming transitions.

Chunking and Breaking Tasks: Break down complex tasks and assignments into smaller, manageable steps to help students with ADHD approach tasks more effectively. Provide checklists, graphic organizers, or written instructions to guide students through multi-step tasks and assignments.

Extended Time and Flexible Deadlines: Allow students with ADHD extended time to complete assignments, tests, or classroom activities to accommodate processing speed and executive functioning challenges. Provide flexibility with deadlines and due dates, offering opportunities for students to submit work in stages or receive partial credit for incomplete assignments.

Support for Organization and Materials Management: Teach organizational skills such as using binders, folders, and planners to help students with ADHD manage materials, assignments, and deadlines. Provide designated storage spaces and organization systems for students to keep track of their belongings and school supplies.

Positive Reinforcement and Rewards: Implement a system of positive reinforcement and rewards to recognize and reinforce desired behaviors and academic achievements. Use praise, encouragement, and tangible rewards such as stickers, tokens, or privilege passes to motivate students and promote a positive learning environment.

Frequent Breaks and Movement Opportunities: Incorporate frequent breaks and movement opportunities throughout the school day to allow students with ADHD to release excess energy and maintain focus. Provide opportunities for physical activity, sensory breaks, or movement-based learning activities to support students' sensory and motor needs.

Clear and Concise Instructions: Provide clear and concise instructions for tasks, assignments, and classroom activities, avoiding ambiguous language or open-ended questions. Break instructions into short, sequential steps and repeat them as needed to ensure understanding and comprehension.

Peer Support and Collaboration: Encourage peer support and collaboration by pairing students with ADHD with peer buddies or study partners who can provide assistance, encouragement, and social support. Foster a classroom culture of inclusivity, empathy, and respect, promoting positive peer relationships and acceptance of individual differences.

Communication and Collaboration with Parents: Maintain open and regular communication with parents and caregivers of students with ADHD, sharing updates on academic progress, behavior, and any concerns or observations. Collaborate with parents to develop and implement effective strategies and supports that align with the student's needs and prcferences.

By implementing these classroom accommodations and modifications, educators can create an inclusive and supportive learning environment where students with ADHD can thrive academically, socially, and emotionally. It's essential to individualize accommodations based on each student's unique strengths, challenges, and preferences, fostering a sense of belonging and empowerment in the classroom.

3.4 Strategies for Homework and Study Skills

Developing effective homework and study skills is crucial for students with ADHD to manage their academic responsibilities and succeed in school. Here are some strategies to support students with ADHD in improving their homework and study skills:

Establish a Consistent Routine: Help students establish a consistent homework routine by setting aside specific times each day for homework and study sessions. Consistency helps create predictability and structure, making it easier for students to manage their time effectively.

Break Tasks into Manageable Steps: Break down homework assignments and study tasks into smaller, more manageable steps. Provide students with clear instructions and checklists to help them stay organized and focused on one task at a time.

Use Visual Organizers and Timelines: Utilize visual organizers, such as charts, calendars, and timelines, to help students plan, prioritize, and track their homework assignments and study goals. Visual aids provide structure and visual cues to assist students in managing their time and tasks effectively.

Minimize Distractions: Create a distraction-free homework environment by minimizing noise, clutter, and electronic distractions. Encourage students to work in a quiet, well-lit area away from televisions, computers, and other distractions that may interfere with their concentration.

Provide Regular Breaks: Incorporate regular breaks into homework and study sessions to help students recharge and maintain focus. Encourage students to take short breaks every 20-30 minutes to stretch, move around, or engage in a brief relaxation activity.

Implement the "5-Minute Rule": Encourage students to start their homework or study tasks with a commitment to work on them for just 5 minutes. Often, getting started is the hardest part, and once students overcome the initial resistance, they may find it easier to continue working.

Teach Time Management Skills: Teach students time management techniques, such as estimating task durations, setting realistic goals, and using timers or alarms to monitor their progress. Help students prioritize tasks based on deadlines and importance to ensure they allocate their time effectively.

Encourage Self-Advocacy: Teach students to advocate for themselves by asking for clarification, seeking help when needed, and communicating their needs to teachers and parents. Encourage students to ask questions, express concerns, and seek support in managing their homework and study workload.

Provide Positive Reinforcement and Support: Offer praise, encouragement, and positive reinforcement to students for their efforts, progress, and accomplishments in completing homework assignments and studying for exams. Celebrate their successes and provide support and guidance when they encounter challenges.

Promote Self-Reflection and Problem-Solving: Encourage students to reflect on their homework and study habits, identify strategies that work best for them, and adjust their approach as needed. Teach problem-solving skills to help students overcome obstacles and develop resilience in the face of academic challenges.

By implementing these strategies and providing ongoing support and guidance, educators and parents can help students with ADHD develop effective homework and study skills, improve academic performance, and build confidence in their ability to succeed academically.

Chapter 4: Behavioral Interventions

- **4.1 Positive Reinforcement and Behavior Charts**
- **4.2 Setting Clear Expectations and Boundaries**
- **4.3 Managing Impulsivity and Emotional Regulation 4.4 Addressing Oppositional Behaviors**

4.1 Positive Reinforcement and Behavior Charts

conduct charts and positive reinforcement are useful tools for encouraging good conduct and inspiring students—including those with ADHD—to meet objectives and follow rules. These methods include visual monitoring, incentives, and praise to reinforce success and promote desirable behaviors. The following are some successful ways to use behavior charts and positive reinforcement:

Determine Target Behaviors: Clearly state the particular behaviors or objectives you want to support. Pay attention to actions that are quantifiable, observable, and doable. Performing homework, adhering to school regulations, maintaining concentration while working on assignments, and using suitable social skills are a few examples.

Create a Reward System: Choose the kinds of incentives or awards that will inspire the pupil. Rewards might be as basic as verbal commendation and encouraging words or as concrete as stickers, tokens, rights, or activities that one prefers. To get the most out of the incentives, make sure they suit the student's interests and preferences.

Make a conduct Chart: To monitor a student's development and encourage good conduct, make a visual behavior chart. The chart must be straightforward, simple to comprehend, and clearly posted at the student's house or school so they may routinely view it. Utilize a checklist or grid to document the student's actions and development over time.

Clarify Your Expectations: Make it clear what is expected of the target behaviors and how incentives are to be earned. Make sure the pupil knows exactly what is expected of them and how their behaviors might result in rewards. To make expectations clear, provide instances and illustrations of the expected actions.

Create a Reward Schedule: Choose how often the learner will be rewarded in accordance with their achievements and growth. To constantly reinforce desirable actions, start with a continuous reinforcement program. To keep the learner motivated and engaged, progressively switch to a flexible reinforcement schedule as the student gains proficiency.

Track and Monitor Progress: Throughout the day or week, keep an eye on the student's conduct by using the behavior chart. Urge the pupil to take an active role in monitoring their own development and self-reflective conduct. Encourage and provide comments to the pupil according to their performance.

Celebrate Successes: On a regular basis, recognize and celebrate the accomplishments of the students. When a student displays the desired behaviors or meets their objectives, give them real praise, encouragement, and prizes. Draw attention to certain actions and initiatives that have helped them succeed.

As necessary, adjust and modify: Track the behavior chart's and reward system efficacy over time. Be adaptable and ready to change the system in response to the requirements, interests, and advancement of the students. As necessary, alter the requirements for receiving incentives, the kinds of prizes given, or the frequency of reinforcement to sustain motivation and encourage ongoing progress.

Engage Parents and Caregivers: Work together with parents and caregivers to establish clear expectations and techniques for positive reinforcement in the household. Provide details regarding the student's development and exhort parents to uphold and reinforce the desired habits at home.

Teach Self-Regulation Skills: Students may learn self-regulation skills and self-monitoring strategies by using behavior charts as a teaching tool. Students should be encouraged to accept responsibility for their acts, reflect on their conduct, and create personal objectives. Give pupils the freedom to choose well and control their own conduct.

Teachers and parents can establish a helpful and inspiring environment that supports and motivates students with ADHD to develop positive behaviors, enhance self-regulation skills, and succeed academically and socially by carefully and consistently implementing behavior charts and positive reinforcement.

4.2 Setting Clear Expectations and Boundaries

Creating a regulated and encouraging environment for kids with ADHD requires clearly defining expectations and limits. Children who have clear expectations are better able to navigate their environment and comprehend what is expected of them. Clear expectations also give stability, predictability, and direction. The following techniques may be used to clearly define limits and expectations for kids with ADHD:

Be Explicit and Concrete: Clearly state your expectations in language that is easy for kids to grasp that is straightforward and precise. Provide specific examples to support the intended behaviors or results instead of giving directions that are unclear or imprecise.

Emphasize Positive Behaviors: Instead of concentrating just on what kids shouldn't do, highlight positive behaviors and desired results.

By emphasizing the actions you want to see and supporting them with encouragement and praise, you may positively frame expectations.

Be Consistent in places: Uphold uniformity in limits and expectations in many contexts, such as the family, school, and other places. Work together with the child's educators, caretakers, and other adults to establish expectations and reinforce good conduct in a cohesive manner.

Establish Developmentally Appropriate objectives: Set age- and skill-appropriate, realistic, and attainable objectives for your kid. Divide more ambitious objectives into more doable, smaller stages so that kids may gradually achieve achievement and gain confidence.

Employ Visual Supports: To assist kids comprehend and remember the rules and routines, provide them with visual aids like charts, diagrams, and visual timetables. Visual aids provide tangible signals and reminders to direct behavior and encourage self-sufficiency.

Set an Example for Expected Behaviors: Set an example for the attitudes and actions you want from kids. In your relationships with other people, show empathy, tolerance, and respect. You should also communicate well to settle disputes and deal with difficulties in a positive way.

Establish Unambiguous Consequences: Make sure that everyone understands the repercussions of both good and bad conduct. Then, always carry out the necessary actions when expectations are fulfilled or not. Make sure the penalties are reasonable, equitable, and in line with the offense.

Promote Self-Regulation and Problem-handling: Give kids the tools they need to become self-regulatory and adept at handling problems by letting them come up with solutions on their own for difficulties and disputes. Children should be taught coping mechanisms for controlling their impulses, emotions, and behavior in a variety of contexts.

Give good Reinforcement: To support good actions and endeavors, give acknowledgment, incentives, and praise. Honor successes and significant anniversaries, and recognize advancements made in relation to expectations. Children that get positive reinforcement are more likely to persist in exhibiting desirable actions.

Regularly Review and Modify Expectations: To make sure that limits and expectations are still appropriate and useful, discuss them with kids on a regular basis. Allow children to give you feedback, and be prepared to modify your expectations in light of their needs, preferences, and developmental stage.

Children with ADHD may benefit from an organized and supportive environment that fosters good behavior, self-regulation, and social-emotional development. This can be achieved by caregivers and educators establishing clear expectations and limits. Effective expectation-setting techniques must include consistency, clarity, and positive reinforcement as essential elements.

4.3 Managing Impulsivity and Emotional Regulation

Children with ADHD need to learn how to control their impulses and emotions in order to successfully navigate social situations, control their conduct, and excel in school. The following techniques may assist kids with ADHD in controlling their impulses and emotions:

Techniques for Relaxation and Mindfulness: Teach kids mindfulness practices to help them relax their bodies and minds when they feel strong emotions or urges. These practices include guided imagery, deep breathing exercises, and body scans. To encourage relaxation and lower levels of stress and anxiety, practice relaxation methods like progressive muscle relaxation and visualization.

Think Things Through Before Acting: Teach kids to consider things through before impulsively acting. Encourage them to pause, reflect on the implications of their actions, and come up with a better, more flexible solution. Make use of visual cues or reminders, such hand signals or stop signs, to encourage kids to think things through before acting on impulse.

Expand Your Self-Awareness: Assist kids in becoming more self-aware by teaching them to identify and categorize their feelings. Instruct them to recognize the bodily sensations and emotional indicators linked to certain emotions, such rage, irritation, or enthusiasm. Encourage kids to voice their demands and concerns in a positive way and to express their emotions vocally.

Exercise Your Problem-Solving Ability: Instruct kids in problem-solving techniques so they can handle difficult circumstances and disputes with grace. Urge them to define the issue, generate potential fixes, weigh the pros and disadvantages, and decide on the best course of action. Play out various scenarios and assist kids in addressing problems to help them gain competence and confidence in handling challenging circumstances.

Make Use of Timers and Visual Aids: Give kids visual aids to help them keep organized and follow routines, such as cue cards, checklists, and visual timetables. Visual aids function as suggestions and reminders to control behavior and lessen impulsivity. Utilize countdown clocks or timers to assist kids in managing their time and maintaining concentration on assignments. Children can better pace themselves and sustain attention when activities are divided into smaller, more manageable pieces and have time constraints.

Promote constructive coping mechanisms: Instruct kids on constructive coping mechanisms to control their impulsivity, tension, and irritation. Encourage healthy avenues for letting off steam, such as physical activity, painting, music, or time spent outside. Assist kids in determining which coping mechanisms, such writing, painting, or talking to a friend or trusted adult, are most effective for them.

Organize and Make Predictable: Establish a routine, norms, and expectations that are consistent and organized. Give kids the chance to help create rules for the classroom or the family by setting clear expectations and standards for conduct. To help kids anticipate changes and efficiently manage their time, use graphic timetables and clocks. Before making any transitions or adjustments to your activity, provide warnings and early notice.

Exhibit Calm and Regulated Conduct: Set an example of composure and self-control while interacting with kids. When faced with difficult circumstances, show self-control, empathy, and tolerance. You may also encourage good actions by using positive words and nonverbal signals. Give kids the chance to see and absorb knowledge from wholesome role models who possess the ability to regulate their emotions and impulses.

Encourage an Environment of Understanding and Support: Establish a kind and understanding atmosphere where kids may freely express their feelings and ask for assistance when they need it. Promote candid dialogue and nonjudgmentally acknowledge the emotions and experiences of kids. Establish trustworthy bonds of acceptance, respect, and empathy with kids. As they develop their ability to control their impulsivity and emotional regulation, pay attention to their wants and concerns and provide advice and support.

Seek Expert Assistance When Necessary: Seek advice and help from mental health specialists, such as psychologists, counselors, or therapists, when dealing with issues related to impulsivity and emotional control. Work together with special education or school counseling staff to create interventions and specific support plans that are suited to each child's needs.

Caregivers, educators, and mental health professionals may assist children with ADHD in developing critical skills for successfully controlling impulsivity and regulating their emotions by putting these ideas into practice and offering ongoing support and advice. Children may learn to overcome obstacles and succeed in a variety of areas of their life with the right kind of support, understanding, and guidance.

4.4   Addressing   Oppositional Behaviors

Children who exhibit oppositional behaviors, including those with ADHD, need to be addressed with a comprehensive and supportive strategy that takes into account the underlying causes of these behaviors. The following techniques may assist in addressing oppositional tendencies in kids with ADHD:

Recognize the Fundamental Causes: Give careful thought to the fundamental causes of the child's oppositional actions. These might include issues with emotional management, frustration tolerance, impulse control, sensory sensitivity, or communication problems.

Set Firm but Fair Boundaries and Clear standards: Define clear, consistent standards for conduct and set boundaries that are both fair and firm. Be sure the youngster knows the rationale behind the expectations by communicating rules and consequences in a clear and concise manner.

Employ excellent Reinforcement: When a youngster exhibits acceptable conduct, reward them with praise, treats, and encouragement. This will reinforce their excellent behavior. Pay attention to when the youngster behaves well and give them credit for their efforts and advancement.

Provide Structure and Predictability: Establish Routines and schedules to create a regulated and predictable atmosphere that will help the youngster feel safe and know what to anticipate. Transitions may be supported and anxiety can be decreased by using visual timetables, timers, and reminders.

Give the youngster Options and Autonomy: Give the youngster the chance to exercise autonomy and make decisions within sensible bounds. Whenever feasible, provide alternatives to the youngster so they may feel in charge of and take responsibility for their choices.

Teach the kid to Solve Problems: Give the kid problem-solving techniques to assist them deal with difficulties and disagreements in an effective manner. Urge them to think through the ramifications, find solutions, and assertively express what they need.

Encourage Emotional Regulation: Provide the youngster with techniques for controlling their feelings and finding healthy methods to deal with frustration and rage. Promote mindfulness, deep breathing, and relaxation methods to assist the youngster in calming down when they are feeling upset.

Employ Proactive tactics: To avoid or reduce disputes, anticipate circumstances that can set off oppositional behaviors and put proactive tactics into place. Make adjustments to the surroundings, give more assistance, or suggest activities that will keep the youngster interested and concentrated.

Model Positive conduct: Give the youngster the opportunity to see and learn from your positive conduct and skillful dispute resolution techniques. In your conversations, show tolerance, compassion, and respect. Steer clear of power battles and developing confrontations.

Seek Professional Assistance: For extra assistance and direction in managing oppositional behaviors, speak with mental health experts such as therapists, counselors, or behavioral specialists. Work together to create a coordinated plan of action to address the child's needs with the help of the school staff and other caregivers.

Emphasis on Developing Relationships: Establish a connection of empathy, respect, and understanding with the kid that is founded on trust and support. Encourage honest dialogue and pay attention to the child's point of view, acknowledging their emotions and experiences.

Handle Underlying Needs: Take into account the possibility that the child's oppositional actions are a reaction to unfulfilled needs or underlying problems, such anxiety, trauma, or learning disabilities. Use the right support and actions to address these needs.

Through the constant and compassionate use of these tactics, mental health professionals, educators, and caregivers may assist children with ADHD in improving their social skills, reducing oppositional behaviors, and developing better coping mechanisms over time. In order to assist the youngster flourish, it's critical to approach them with empathy and understanding while also offering strong advice and support.

Chapter 5: Medication and Alternative Treatments

- **5.1 Understanding ADHD Medications**
- **5.2 Exploring Alternative Treatments and Therapies**
- **5.3 Complementary Approaches: Diet, Exercise, and Sleep**

5.1 Understanding ADHD Medications

Understanding ADHD medications is essential for individuals diagnosed with Attention-Deficit/Hyperactivity Disorder (ADHD), as well as their caregivers and healthcare providers. ADHD medications are commonly prescribed to help manage symptoms such as inattention, hyperactivity, and impulsivity. Here is an overview of ADHD medications and how they work:

Stimulant Medications:

- Stimulant medications are the most commonly prescribed treatment for ADHD and are considered first-line therapy for managing symptoms.

- They work by increasing the levels of neurotransmitters, such as dopamine and norepinephrine, in the brain, which play a key role in regulating attention, focus, and impulse control.

The two main types of stimulant medications used to treat ADHD are:

1. **Methylphenidate:** Examples include Ritalin, Concerta, Metadate, and Daytrana (patch).

2. **Amphetamines:** Examples include Adderall, Vyvanse, Dexedrine, and Evekeo.

Non-Stimulant Medications:

- Non-stimulant medications are another option for treating ADHD, particularly for individuals who do not respond well to or cannot tolerate stimulant medications.

- They work by targeting different neurotransmitters and brain pathways compared to stimulant medications.

Examples of non-stimulant medications used to treat ADHD include:

1. Atomoxetine (Strattera)

2. Guanfacine (Intuniv)

3. Clonidine (Kapvay)

How ADHD Medications Help:

- ADHD medications help improve attention, focus, impulse control, and executive function skills, allowing individuals to better manage daily tasks, schoolwork, work responsibilities, and social interactions.

- They can also reduce hyperactivity, impulsivity, and disruptive behaviors associated with ADHD, leading to improved functioning and quality of life.

Dosage and Administration:

- ADHD medications are typically available in various forms, including tablets, capsules, chewable tablets, extended-release capsules, and patches.

- The dosage and administration schedule depend on the specific medication, the individual's age, weight, and symptom severity, as well as their response to treatment.

- It is important to follow the healthcare provider's instructions carefully and adhere to the prescribed dosage and schedule to optimize treatment outcomes and minimize potential side effects.

Side Effects:

Common side effects of ADHD medications may include:

- Decreased appetite and weight loss

- Sleep disturbances

- Increased heart rate and blood pressure

- Headaches

- Irritability or mood swings

Most side effects are mild and temporary, but individuals should report any concerning or persistent side effects to their healthcare provider.

Monitoring and Follow-Up:

- Regular monitoring and follow-up with a healthcare provider are essential when taking ADHD medications.

- Healthcare providers may adjust the dosage, switch medications, or modify the treatment plan based on the individual's response to medication and any side effects experienced.

- It is important to communicate openly with the healthcare provider and report any changes in symptoms or concerns related to medication treatment.

Comprehensive Treatment Approach:

- Medication treatment is often part of a comprehensive approach to managing ADHD that may include behavioral therapy, educational interventions, lifestyle modifications, and support from family, educators, and mental health professionals.

- Individualized treatment plans take into account the unique needs, strengths, and preferences of each individual with ADHD.

It's important for individuals and their families to work closely with healthcare providers to develop a treatment plan that addresses their specific needs and goals. By understanding how ADHD medications work and their potential benefits and risks, individuals can make informed decisions about their treatment and

take an active role in managing their ADHD
symptoms.

5.2 Exploring Alternative Treatments and Therapies

Those who would prefer non-medication techniques or want to supplement established treatments for ADHD may find more possibilities by researching alternative therapies and treatments. Alternative therapies may be useful elements of an all-encompassing treatment approach, even if they might not be able to replace evidence-based methods. Here are a few different therapies and treatments for ADHD:

Behavioral Intervention: In order to control symptoms and enhance functioning, behavioral treatment—such as cognitive-behavioral therapy (CBT) and behavior modification approaches—can teach people with ADHD coping mechanisms, self-regulation techniques, and problem-solving methods.

The main goals of behavioral therapy are to improve social interactions and relationships, lessen impulsivity, enhance organizational abilities, and change certain habits.

Education and Training for Parents: Parent-Child Interaction Therapy (PCIT) and the Incredible Years program are two examples of parent education programs that provide parents the skills and techniques they need to successfully manage their child's behavior and ADHD symptoms.

Through these programs, parents may learn how to manage difficult behaviors at home and in other contexts, as well as set clear expectations, create routines, and use positive reinforcement.

Interventions Based on Mindfulness: Increased self-awareness, attentional control, and emotional regulation may be achieved by people with ADHD via mindfulness exercises including tai chi, yoga, and mindfulness meditation.

Individuals undergoing mindfulness-based therapies learn to create a feeling of peace and balance, notice their thoughts and emotions without passing judgment, and concentrate their attention on the present moment.

Physical activity and exercise: For those with ADHD, regular exercise and physical activity may help lower hyperactivity, increase focus and attention, and improve general well being.

Sports, dancing, swimming, bicycling, and martial arts are a few examples of hobbies that might provide chances for social connection, stress relief, and self-expression.

Interventions related to nutrition: Although studies on the connection between nutrition and ADHD are still underway, some people may benefit from dietary modifications or supplements. According to some research, diets high in antioxidants, vitamins, minerals, and omega-3 fatty acids may help people with

ADHD maintain their brain health and cognitive performance.

Speaking with a qualified dietitian or nutritionist may assist people in investigating dietary options and identifying any triggers or food sensitivities that can aggravate symptoms of ADHD.

Both neurofeedback and biofeedback: Neurofeedback and biofeedback methods track and modify brainwave activity to help ADHD sufferers become more focused, attentive, and self-aware.

With the assistance of digital technology, these methods teach people how to modify their brain activity via practice and reinforcement, as well as real-time feedback on brainwave patterns.

Expressive therapies, including art therapy: People with ADHD may explore and express their feelings, ideas, and experiences via creative outlets provided by expressive therapies such as music therapy, art therapy, and others.

While participating in creative endeavors like writing, music, painting, and sketching, these treatments may support the development of coping mechanisms, self-expression, and self-esteem in patients.

Changes to the Environment: Making adjustments to their surroundings, such as cutting down on distractions, setting up routines, and organizing rooms, may help people with ADHD better handle sensory overload and increase productivity.

Providing visual timetables, checklists, and organizing tools may help people remain focused and efficiently manage their daily duties.

Instruction in Social Skills: Programs for developing social skills educate people with ADHD how to improve their interpersonal connections and social interactions by teaching them critical social skills including collaboration, empathy, communication, and problem-solving.

People may acquire and use social skills in a variety of social contexts with the aid of role-playing, modeling, and supervised practice.

Comprehensive Methods: Complementary therapies for ADHD symptoms include holistic practices including aromatherapy, herbal medicine, and acupuncture.

Even though there is no data to support the efficacy of these strategies, some people may benefit from holistic therapies by feeling better overall or with specific ailments.

It's crucial to remember that alternative therapies and treatments have to be used in concert with evidence-based interventions and under the supervision of licensed medical practitioners.

Individuals with ADHD may safely and effectively research and incorporate alternative therapies into their entire treatment plan by consulting with healthcare experts, therapists, and specialists. Furthermore, continuous assessment and observation are necessary to determine the efficacy of

5.3 Complementary Approaches: Diet, Exercise, and Sleep

For those with ADHD, complementary therapies including nutrition, exercise, and sleep may be crucial in controlling symptoms and enhancing general wellbeing. These methods may enhance other interventions and lead to better results, even if they might not completely replace conventional therapies. For those with ADHD, the following lifestyle, exercise, and sleep modifications might be helpful:

Nutritional Points to Remember:

Cognitive function and brain function are significantly influenced by nutrition. Although there isn't a single "ADHD diet," there are dietary elements that may have an influence on symptoms and general health.

Promote a nutritious, well-balanced diet that is high in whole grains, fruits, vegetables, lean meats, and healthy fats. Reduce your intake of artificial chemicals, sugary snacks, and processed meals.

According to some study, people with ADHD may benefit from taking fish oil, which contains omega-3 fatty acids, as well as vitamins and minerals including iron, magnesium, and zinc. Think about include foods high in these nutrients in your diet.

Keep an eye out for dietary intolerances or sensitivities that can make symptoms of ADHD worse. Dairy, gluten, artificial coloring, and preservatives are common offenders. Maintaining a meal journal might assist in determining possible triggers.

For individualized nutritional advice, speak with a qualified dietitian or nutritionist.

Frequent Workout:

- It has been shown that for those with ADHD, physical exercise improves executive function, attention, and mood management.

- Promote frequent physical activity and exercise as a component of a healthy lifestyle. Exercise and stress alleviation may be obtained by participating in sports, walking, jogging, bicycling, swimming, dancing, and team walking.

- For children and adolescents, try to get at least 60 minutes a day of moderate to intense physical exercise; for adults, aim for 150 minutes a week.

- To enhance physical fitness and general well-being, include exercise in everyday routines and promote outdoor play and leisure pursuits.

Good Sleep Practices:

- Getting enough sleep is critical for maintaining emotional stability, cognitive function, and general wellness. Sleep disruptions and abnormal sleep patterns may be more common in children and adults diagnosed with ADHD.

- Even on weekends, stick to a regular sleep routine that includes set bedtimes and wake-up hours.

- Establish a calming sleep ritual to let your body know when it's time to relax. Before going to bed, stay away from screens, electronics, and stimulating activities.

- Establish a peaceful, dark, and comfortable sleeping space that promotes deep, restful sleep. To reduce distractions, think about using blackout curtains or white noise generators.

- Under the supervision of a healthcare provider, keep an eye on your sleep patterns and take care of any sleep issues or disorders, such as insomnia, restless legs syndrome, or sleep apnea.

- Make good sleep hygiene a priority. This includes cutting down on coffee, avoiding large meals right before bed, and using relaxation methods to help you go asleep and stay asleep.

People may improve their health, well-being, and symptom management by combining these complementary strategies into their overall ADHD treatment strategy. It's crucial to confer with medical professionals, therapists, and experts in order to create a thorough treatment plan that takes into account the particular requirements and preferences of every person with ADHD. Furthermore, continuous assessment and observation may assist in tracking progress and modifying treatment plans as necessary.

Chapter 6: Supporting Social and Emotional Development

- **6.1 Building Self-Esteem and Confidence**
- **6.2 Navigating Social Relationships**
- **6.3 Coping with Frustration and Rejection**
- **6.4 Encouraging Healthy Peer Interactions**

6.1 Building Self-Esteem and Confidence

Developing self-worth and self-assurance is crucial for anyone, especially those with ADHD, to create a good self-concept, overcome obstacles, and succeed in a variety of spheres of life. The following techniques may assist people with ADHD in developing confidence and self-worth:

Honor Your Strengths and Achievements: Motivate others to acknowledge and appreciate their accomplishments, skills, and abilities. Highlight their accomplishments, no matter how little, and concentrate on their special abilities, talents, and good traits. Reward efforts and successes with targeted praise and encouraging comments. Acknowledge their development over time and convey your belief in their capacity to overcome obstacles.

Establish Achievable and Realistic Goals: Assist people in establishing achievable, realistic objectives that are consistent with their beliefs, interests, and ambitions. Divide more ambitious objectives into more doable, smaller ones in order to create momentum and a feeling of success. People should be encouraged to create challenging but attainable objectives for themselves. Encourage, mentor, and assist them as they strive toward their objectives.

Promote Self-Revelation and Originality: Make time for creative expression and self-expression by engaging in hobbies, music, painting, and writing. People should be encouraged to follow their passions, be genuine in their expression, and engage in happy, fulfilling activities. Create a welcoming and nonjudgmental atmosphere where people can freely express their ideas, emotions, and opinions without worrying about being accepted or criticized.

Encourage resilience and problem-solving skills: Teach people how to solve problems and develop resilience so they can deal with obstacles and failures in a healthy way. Urge them to see challenges as chances for development and learning rather than as roadblocks to achievement. Assist people in recognizing their assets and talents, generate ideas for possible solutions, and create action plans to deal with problems and go over barriers. Be a resilient and persistent role model for others by modeling optimism, flexibility, and a positive outlook in the face of difficulty.

Promote Confident Thoughts for Yourself: Encourage the use of empowering phrases and positive affirmations to combat self-limiting ideas and negative self-talk. Urge people to replace pessimistic ideas about themselves with positive ones that reinforce their value, skills, and potential. Assist others in developing self-acceptance and self-compassion by showing them love, understanding, and forgiving toward themselves. Urge them to show themselves the same kindness and understanding that they show others.

Encourage Support and Social Connections: Assist people in developing wholesome social bonds and interactions with mentors, family members, peers, and caring adults. Promote deep conversations, teamwork, and shared experiences that strengthen a feeling of acceptance and belonging. Give them the chance to join clubs, support groups, community organizations, and group activities so they may meet others with similar interests and backgrounds.

Encourage self-reliance and autonomy: Motivate people to be self-reliant, make decisions, and accept responsibility for their deeds. Give them the chance to be independent and autonomous when making decisions, solving problems, and creating goals. Provide direction and assistance when required, but let people make errors, grow from their experiences, and gain confidence in their capacity to function on their own in the world.

Seek Expert Assistance When Necessary: Urge them to seek out professional help from coaches, therapists, or counselors who specialize in self-esteem, confidence development, and ADHD. Professional counseling and guidance may provide insightful information, practical tactics, and encouragement to help people on their path to improved confidence and self-worth.

Through the use of these techniques and the provision of continuous support and motivation, mental health professionals, educators, and caregivers may facilitate the development of resilience, self-worth, and confidence in persons with ADHD. Although gaining self-worth and confidence is a slow and continuous process that calls for tolerance, understanding, and empathy, the rewards are enormous and provide people a great sense of empowerment as they face life's obstacles and seize its possibilities.

6.2 Navigating Social Relationships

For those with ADHD, navigating social interactions may be enjoyable and difficult at the same time. Problems with focus, impulsivity, and social skills might hinder their capacity to establish and maintain deep relationships with others. However, people with ADHD are capable of forming fulfilling social interactions if they are given the right knowledge, assistance, and practice. The following techniques may be used to manage social relationships:

Gain Social Skills: Instruct and exercise social skills including empathy, perspective-taking, active listening, and turn-taking. Play out typical social situations and provide advice on suitable replies.

Provide direction on nonverbal indicators of communication, such tone of voice, body language, facial expressions, and eye contact. People should be encouraged to practice striking up discussions, asking inquiries, and participating in group activities.

Become More Self-Aware: Promote self-awareness development in people with ADHD by having them reflect on their own emotions, ideas, and actions in social contexts.

Talk about your social connections' positives and negatives, and come up with solutions to problems and ways to improve. Urge people to acknowledge the feelings they are experiencing as well as those of others, and to think about the effects of their actions on others around them.

Control your hyperactivity and impulsivity: Provide techniques for controlling hyperactivity and impulsivity in social situations. Encourage people to adopt relaxation methods to lessen tension and anxiety, to take long breaths to calm themselves, and to stop and consider their responses before speaking. In order to better concentrate during social interactions and help channel surplus energy, provide chances for physical exercise and movement breaks.

Develop Your Perspective-Taking Skills: Assist people with ADHD in comprehending various viewpoints and opinions. Motivate them to think about what other people may be thinking or feeling in a certain circumstance and to be empathetic and understanding of other people's perspectives.

Take part in activities that encourage perspective-taking, such role-playing various events from various points of view or talking about the motives of characters in novels or films.

Look for shared interests: Urge people to look for events and communities where they may interact with others who have similar interests to their own. Getting involved in clubs, sports teams, hobby groups, or community organizations may help you meet others who share your interests.

Encourage connections based on principles, interests, and pastimes in common. Urge people to find others who share their hobbies and to engage in things they like.

Cultivate Optimal Connections: Stress the value of forming wholesome and encouraging relationships with family, friends, and mentors. Urge people to engage with others in a courteous, inclusive, and friendly manner.

Instruct students in constructive conflict resolution and dispute management techniques. Promote compromise, open conversation, and attentive listening while settling disputes.

Offer Social Assistance and Counseling: Help people with ADHD manage social connections by providing them with social support and direction. Make yourself accessible to listen, counsel, and critique social interactions.

Assist people in finding dependable companions and mentors who can provide assistance, motivation, and direction in interacting with others.

Seek Expert Assistance When Necessary: Urge those suffering from ADHD to get help from therapists, counselors, or social skills organizations that focus on helping them with social difficulties. In order to assist people become more confident, manage social connections more skillfully, and enhance their social skills, professional support may provide methods, resources, and tools.

Through the use of these tactics and the provision of continuous support and motivation, mental health professionals, educators, and caregivers may assist persons with ADHD in acquiring the social skills and self-assurance required to effectively navigate social interactions. For those with ADHD, establishing strong social ties may improve their general quality of life, wellbeing, and sense of self-worth.

6.3 Coping with Frustration and Rejection

Anyone might find it difficult to cope with frustration and rejection, but those with ADHD may have particular problems because they struggle with impulse control, emotional regulation, and social relationships. Nonetheless, there are a number of techniques that may improve how well people with ADHD handle rejection and frustration:

Acknowledge and Give Meaning to Emotions: Urge those who suffer from ADHD to identify and accept their emotions of annoyance and rejection. Reassure them that it's OK to feel angry or let down when faced with difficult circumstances by validating their feelings.

Use relaxation and mindfulness techniques: Instruct people with ADHD in mindfulness practices like progressive muscle relaxation, deep breathing, and meditation to help them relax their bodies and minds when they feel rejected or upset. These methods may aid in fostering serenity and lowering mental anguish.

Promote Efficient Communication: Urge people who have ADHD to communicate their emotions and ideas in a productive way. Show children how to assertively express their wants and feelings using "I" statements without placing blame or drawing criticism.

Concentrate on Finding Solutions: Assist people in changing their attention from focusing on the issue at hand to considering possible solutions. Urge them to come up with doable solutions for dealing with the circumstance and taking a constructive step ahead.

Develop Your Resilience: Encourage resilience by stressing the value of tenacity and overcoming obstacles. Assist people in reframing rejection as a chance for development and education rather than a reflection on their value or competence.

Promote Self-Compassion: People should learn to treat themselves with kindness and compassion, even when they are rejected or fail. Remind them that self-compassion is a crucial component of resilience and that everyone has setbacks.

Ask for Assistance from Others: Urge those who need advice and encouragement during trying times to get in touch with friends, family, or mental health specialists. Reassurance and validation may be obtained via having a robust support system.

Have Reasonable Expectations: Assist people in having reasonable expectations of both themselves and other people. Urge children to applaud their accomplishments, no matter how little, and to place more emphasis on progress than perfection.

Take Care of Yourself: Urge people to place a high priority on self-care practices that enhance their mental and physical health, such as getting regular exercise, eating a balanced diet, getting enough sleep, and taking up hobbies or enjoyable activities.

Create Coping Mechanisms: Collaborate with people to determine the most effective coping mechanisms for them in handling frustration and rejection. These may include taking a vacation, doing something you like, keeping a diary, or getting help from a professional.

Demonstrate Good Coping Strategies: In your personal interactions and reactions, provide an example for constructive coping mechanisms and constructive approaches to handling frustration and rejection. Resilience and problem-solving abilities shown may provide a great example for others to follow.

With the use of these techniques and continued assistance, people with ADHD may learn useful coping mechanisms to deal with rejection and frustration in more positive and healthy ways. It's crucial to understand that coping mechanisms might differ from person to person, so encourage those in need to find the ones that suit them the most.

6.4 Encouraging Healthy Peer Interactions

Fostering positive peer relationships is crucial for helping people with ADHD become more socially adept, form friendships, and feel included in their peer group. The following are some methods to encourage constructive peer relationships for people with ADHD:

Give Social Skills Instruction: Provide group therapy sessions or social skills training programs that teach people with ADHD basic social skills including taking turns, active listening, striking up discussions, and peacefully resolving problems. Practice social skills in a safe, controlled setting by using role-playing games and real-world situations.

Provide Socialization Opportunities: Plan social gatherings, organizations, or group activities where people with ADHD may engage with others who have similar interests and pastimes. Giving people organized interaction chances might make them feel more at ease and self-assured in social situations.

Promote involvement in extracurricular activities, athletic teams, or neighborhood associations where people may make new acquaintances and socialize outside of the classroom.

Encourage Acceptance and Inclusion: Promote compassion, empathy, and respect for diversity to create an inclusive and accepting culture in clubs, schools, and other social situations. Urge people to be hospitable and inclusive to peers with different talents, interests, and backgrounds. Encourage non-inclusive conduct, such as taunting and bullying.

Encourage peer support and mentoring: Assign peer mentors or buddies who can provide companionship, support, and direction to those with ADHD. Peer mentors may help people navigate social circumstances by acting as good role models and by offering emotional and social support.

Urge them to look for allies and friends who will accept and understand them for who they are. Creating a network of encouraging peers might make people feel more important and connected.

Instruct Students on Conflict Resolution Techniques: Provide effective conflict resolution and peer dispute management techniques to people with ADHD. Motivate people to resolve problems in a courteous and productive way by using assertive communication, active listening, and problem-solving techniques. Give advice on how to assertively communicate wants and sentiments while being sympathetic and cognizant of other people's viewpoints.

Set a good example for social behavior: As an example of good social conduct and interpersonal skills, set an example for those with ADHD and their peers. In your interactions and communication, show inclusion, empathy, and active listening. When you see someone exhibiting excellent social behaviors—like sharing, collaborating, and being nice to others—give them feedback and praise.

Promote Social Interaction in Small Groups: In smaller gatherings, where they can feel more at ease and less overwhelmed than in larger ones, encourage people with ADHD to engage in social activities and discussions. Provide chances for people to socialize with peers in smaller groups—like study sessions, gaming evenings, or organizations centered around common interests.

Encourage a positive sense of self and self-worth: Assist people with ADHD in cultivating a good sense of self and self-worth by emphasizing their abilities, aptitudes, and distinctive characteristics. Motivate them to enjoy their successes and accept the differences that make them unique. Give people the chance to express their abilities, passions, and contributions in public places to increase their self-esteem and feeling of community.

Teachers, caregivers, and mental health professionals may assist people with ADHD in gaining the social skills and self-assurance necessary to promote positive peer relationships and enduring friendships by putting these ideas into practice and offering continuous support. People's general well-being and social development may be enhanced by fostering an atmosphere that is encouraging and inclusive and makes them feel appreciated and welcomed.

Chapter 7: Family Dynamics and Support

- **7.1 Strengthening Family Relationships**
- **7.2 Providing Emotional Support for Siblings**
- **7.3 Managing Parental Stress and Burnout**
- **7.4 Seeking Support Networks and Resources**

7.1 Strengthening Family Relationships

For people with ADHD, it's critical to build stronger family ties since stable, supportive family dynamics may provide a solid basis for overcoming obstacles and promoting development. When ADHD is present, use these techniques to improve family dynamics:

Knowledge and comprehension: Inform family members about the signs, difficulties, and available treatments for ADHD. Gaining knowledge about the illness helps increase empathy, dispel myths, and encourage practical support techniques.

Promote candid discussion about ADHD-related subjects, emotions, and experiences within the family. Establish a secure environment where people with ADHD may express themselves without worrying about criticism or judgment.

Working Together to Solve Problems: Include family members in cooperative procedures for managing ADHD, such as problem-solving and decision-making. Invite everyone to share their thoughts, opinions, and ideas on how best to help the person with ADHD. Encourage cooperation and shared accountability among family members in handling ADHD-related issues.

Clearly define your routines and expectations: Give people with ADHD structure and stability in the family by establishing clear expectations, guidelines, and routines. Make sure that everyone understands the expectations for conduct, duties, and repercussions. Establish regular plans and routines that support stability, predictability, and structure in the home while also meeting the requirements of those with ADHD.

Engage in Validation and Active Listening: Recognize and affirm one another's ideas, emotions, and experiences as a family to practice active listening and validation. Encourage your family members to listen intently to one another's worries, to express empathy, and to act without passing judgment.

Acknowledge the special difficulties that people with ADHD may encounter and provide empathy and support for them by validating their feelings and experiences.

Honor accomplishments and advancements: Honor the successes, turning points, and advancements achieved by family members and people with ADHD. No matter how modest, appreciate and value their labor, assets, and successes. Establish a welcoming environment for the family that prioritizes resilience, affirmation, and encouragement.

Encourage Bonding Activities and Quality Time: Set aside time for family bonding and quality time as a top priority to build connections and deepen bonds. Arrange frequent movie marathons, game evenings, family vacations, and pastimes that will foster closeness and provide enduring memories. During family activities, promote meaningful relationships and open communication so that everyone may take part and communicate with one another.

Encourage Family and Individual Well-Being: Encourage the well-being of the individual and the family by placing a high priority on stress reduction, self-care, and healthy living. Encourage all members of the family to practice relaxation methods, consume a nutritious diet, and get regular exercise and sleep. Establish a safe space where people may express their feelings, ask for assistance, and take care of both their own and other people's needs.

Seek Expert Assistance When Necessary: Seek for professional assistance from counselors, therapists, or family therapists with expertise in family dynamics and ADHD. Expert advice and counseling may provide helpful resources, tactics, and understanding to support the development of family bonds and the successful negotiation of obstacles.

Think about going to support groups or family therapy sessions where family members may discuss ADHD-related concerns, pick up efficient communication techniques, and create coping mechanisms together.

These techniques may help people with ADHD feel understood, welcomed, and empowered to flourish in their families by creating a loving and caring atmosphere. For those with ADHD, stable, loving connections within the family are essential for helping them deal with life's ups and downs.

7.2 Providing Emotional Support for Siblings

It is crucial to provide emotional support to siblings of people with ADHD in order to foster empathy, understanding, and harmonious family relationships. In relation to their sibling's ADHD, siblings may encounter a variety of feelings and difficulties, such as dissatisfaction, anger, anxiety, and uncertainty. The following are some methods for offering siblings emotional support:

Knowledge and Consciousness: Inform siblings about the signs, difficulties, and effects of ADHD on behavior and interpersonal interactions. Assist them in realizing that their sibling's actions are not deliberate or personal and that ADHD is a neurological disease. Give siblings books, articles, and other age-appropriate materials on ADHD to help them better comprehend their sibling's needs and experiences.

Promote Open Communication: Encourage open communication between siblings by providing a judgment-free, secure space for them to share their ideas, emotions, and worries about matters pertaining to ADHD.

Siblings should be encouraged to express their concerns and disappointments as well as to ask questions and share their experiences. Pay close attention, acknowledge their feelings, and provide compassion and assistance.

Normalize Your Experiences and Feelings: Normalize the emotions and experiences that siblings have when they have an ADHD sibling. Tell them that it's OK to have a variety of feelings, such as love, guilt, rage, envy, and frustration.

Educate siblings on the fact that many other siblings of people with ADHD may have comparable difficulties and sentiments, so they are not alone in their experiences.

Encourage compassion and understanding: Siblings should be encouraged to put themselves in their sibling's shoes and see things from their viewpoint in order to foster empathy and compassion for their ADHD sibling.

Assist siblings in appreciating the special traits and talents of their ADHD brother, and jointly celebrate their accomplishments.

Give each person individualized attention and assistance: To deepen your relationship and promote a feeling of connection and belonging, set aside time for each sibling to get personalized attention and engage in activities.

Give each sibling the chance to follow their own interests and hobbies while also recognizing and appreciating their own abilities, accomplishments, and areas of interest.

Promote Self-Healing and Coping Mechanisms: In order to manage tension, irritation, and other feelings associated with having an ADHD sibling, siblings should be encouraged to emphasize self-care and to adopt appropriate coping mechanisms.

To assist siblings deal with difficult circumstances and emotions, teach them stress management skills, mindfulness exercises, and relaxation techniques.

Set a good example for communication and behavior: Set a good example for the family in terms of conduct and communication techniques, such as active listening, empathy, patience, and handling conflict. Encourage respect and understanding among family members by showing each sibling your undying love, acceptance, and support.

Look for Resources and Assistance: Make connections between siblings and internet forums, support groups, or therapy services designed especially for siblings of people with ADHD. These sites may provide a feeling of belonging, validation, and support from others who have gone through comparable things.

Think about family therapy or counseling sessions, where siblings may build their connections, enhance communication, and explore their emotions in a safe and healing setting.

Through the use of these techniques and continuous emotional support, parents and caregivers may assist siblings of people with ADHD in navigating their experiences with empathy, forbearance, and comprehension. Good sibling relationships may be a great source of companionship, support, and connection for people with ADHD and their siblings as they go through the ups and downs of family life together.

7.3 Managing Parental Stress and Burnout

Since raising an ADHD kid may be very difficult, it's critical for caregivers to manage parental stress and burnout. The following techniques may help parents manage their stress and avoid burnout:

Self-Healing Techniques: Make self-care a priority by scheduling time for pursuits that advance mental, emotional, and physical health. This includes obtaining enough rest, consuming wholesome foods, working out often, and practicing relaxing methods like yoga, meditation, or deep breathing.

Plan frequent downtime and alone time to refresh and regenerate. Stress may be reduced and energy levels can be restored with even brief pauses.

Have Reasonable Expectations: Recognize that raising a kid with ADHD has special difficulties and constraints. Establish reasonable goals for both you and your kid, keeping in mind that failures and a slow pace of advancement are common occurrences.

Aim for attainable objectives and acknowledge little accomplishments along the route. Let's get rid of perfectionism and needless pressure by prioritizing what has to be done, breaking things down into manageable chunks.

Look for Social Assistance: Seek emotional support and understanding from friends, family, online networks, or support groups. Making connections with others who have gone through comparable things may provide comfort, understanding, and useful guidance.

Joining a support group designed for parents of children with ADHD may help you manage the difficulties of ADHD parenting by allowing you to voice your worries, get advice from other parents, and get perspective.

Converse & Work Together: Whether it's your spouse, co-parent, or other caregivers, keep lines of communication open. As a team, share duties, reach decisions, and provide mutual support throughout the highs and lows of parenthood.

Communicate openly about your wants, constraints, and emotions while fostering understanding and support among family members.

Use Stress-Reduction Techniques: To assist you with the responsibilities of parenthood, learn and put stress management strategies into practice. Journaling, progressive muscle relaxation, guided imagery, and mindfulness meditation are a few examples of this.

Determine what stresses you out and create coping mechanisms to deal with them before they become a problem. Acknowledge the significance of self-awareness and self-control in properly handling stress.

Prioritize self-care and establish boundaries: To avoid overload and burnout, establish limits for your time, energy, and resources. Saying no to extra responsibilities or commitments that might add to stress and tiredness is a valuable skill.

Prioritize your own well-being by setting aside time for "me time" and doing things that make you happy and fulfilled. Recall that in order to adequately care for others, you must first take care of yourself.

Seek Expert Assistance When Required: If you're experiencing anxiety, depression, or overwhelming feelings, don't be afraid to get professional treatment. A mental health expert, such as a therapist or counselor, may provide personalized advice, support, and coping mechanisms.

To address family dynamics, communication problems, and stress management techniques within the family unit, think about family therapy or counseling sessions.

Concentrate on the Good: Develop an attitude of thankfulness and concentrate on the advantages of being a parent and your bond with your kid. Remind yourself of your parenting qualities and celebrate your successes and moments of pleasure, connection, and advancement.

You may better manage parental stress and avoid burnout while giving your kid with ADHD the love, support, and direction they need to flourish by putting these methods into practice and placing a high priority on your own well-being. Recall that caring for yourself is not selfishness; rather, it is necessary to enable you to provide long-term, effective care for your kid and family.

7.4 Seeking Support Networks and Resources

Seeking support networks and resources is crucial for parents of children with ADHD to navigate challenges, gain knowledge, and find emotional support. Here are some avenues for finding support:

Local Support Groups: Look for local support groups or organizations dedicated to ADHD and parenting. These groups often provide opportunities for parents to connect with others facing similar challenges, share experiences, and learn from each other's strategies and insights.

Online Communities: Explore online forums, chat groups, and social media communities focused on ADHD and parenting. Websites such as CHADD (Children and Adults with Attention-Deficit/Hyperactivity Disorder) offer online support groups and forums where parents can ask questions, share resources, and connect with other parents and experts.

Parent Training Programs: Consider enrolling in parent training programs or workshops specifically designed for parents of children with ADHD. Programs such as the "Parent Training and Information Centers" (PTIs) provide workshops, webinars, and resources to help parents learn effective strategies for managing ADHD and advocating for their child's needs.

Therapy and Counseling: Seek individual or family therapy with a therapist who specializes in ADHD and family dynamics. Therapy can provide a safe space to explore emotions, learn coping strategies, improve communication, and strengthen family relationships.

Educational Resources: Explore books, articles, and online resources about ADHD and parenting. Look for reputable sources such as books by ADHD experts, academic journals, and websites of recognized organizations like the American Academy of Pediatrics (AAP) and the National Institute of Mental Health (NIMH).

School Support Services: Reach out to your child's school to inquire about support services and resources available for children with ADHD. School psychologists, counselors, and special education teachers can offer guidance, accommodations, and interventions to support your child's academic and social-emotional needs.

Medical Professionals: Consult with pediatricians, child psychiatrists, or developmental pediatricians who specialize in ADHD. They can provide medical evaluations, medication management, and referrals to other specialists as needed. Building a collaborative relationship with your child's healthcare providers is essential for addressing ADHD-related concerns effectively.

Parenting Classes and Workshops: Attend parenting classes, workshops, or seminars that focus on ADHD and behavior management techniques. These classes often provide practical strategies, tips, and resources for managing challenging behaviors, promoting positive discipline, and fostering healthy family dynamics.

Advocacy Organizations: Get involved with advocacy organizations and networks dedicated to ADHD awareness and support. Organizations such as CHADD, ADDitude Magazine, and the ADHD Awareness Coalition advocate for policy changes, raise public awareness, and provide resources for individuals and families affected by ADHD.

Peer Support: Connect with other parents of children with ADHD through informal networks, playgroups, or school events. Building relationships with other parents who understand your experiences can offer validation, empathy, and practical support in navigating the joys and challenges of parenting a child with ADHD.

By tapping into these support networks and resources, parents can access valuable information, guidance, and emotional support to help them effectively support their child with ADHD and promote their overall well-being as a family. Remember that seeking support is a sign of strength and resilience, and you are not alone in your journey as a parent of a child with ADHD.

Chapter 8: Looking Towards the Future

- **8.1 Transitioning to Adolescence and Adulthood**
- **8.2 Building Independence and Life Skills**
- **8.3 Exploring Career and Educational Opportunities**
- **8.4 Advocating for Continued Support and Understanding**

8.1 Transitioning to Adolescence and Adulthood

Transitioning to adolescence and adulthood presents unique challenges for individuals with ADHD and their families. It's a period marked by changes in academic expectations, social dynamics, independence, and self-identity. Here are some strategies to navigate this transition effectively:

Education and Awareness: Educate your child about ADHD and its impact on various aspects of life, including academics, relationships, and self-regulation. Help them understand their strengths, challenges, and the importance of self-advocacy.

Transition Planning: Start transition planning early to prepare your child for the changes and responsibilities associated with adolescence and adulthood. Involve them in discussions about goals, aspirations, and potential challenges they may face.

Collaborate with educators, therapists, and healthcare providers to develop a transition plan that addresses academic, vocational, social, and emotional needs. Consider factors such as college readiness, career exploration, independent living skills, and self-care routines.

Executive Functioning Skills: Teach and reinforce executive functioning skills such as organization, time management, planning, prioritization, and goal setting. Help your child develop strategies for managing tasks, breaking projects into smaller steps, and staying focused and motivated.

Encourage the use of tools and technology (e.g., planners, calendars, reminder apps) to support executive functioning and promote independence.

Self-Advocacy and Communication: Foster your child's ability to self-advocate and communicate their needs effectively. Encourage them to speak up in school, work, and social settings, and to seek accommodations and support when necessary.

Role-play challenging scenarios and practice assertive communication skills, including articulating strengths, expressing concerns, and negotiating solutions with teachers, employers, and peers.

Social Skills Development: Support your child in developing social skills and navigating social relationships during adolescence and adulthood. Provide opportunities for them to practice social interactions, collaborate with peers, and develop friendships based on shared interests and values.

Encourage participation in extracurricular activities, clubs, or community groups where they can connect with like-minded individuals and build a support network.

Emotional Regulation and Coping Strategies: Help your child develop emotional regulation and coping strategies to manage stress, anxiety, and frustration effectively. Teach relaxation techniques, mindfulness practices, and problem-solving skills to promote resilience and well-being.

Encourage open communication about emotions and offer support and validation during challenging times. Model healthy coping mechanisms and provide a safe space for your child to express themselves without judgment.

Transitioning to College or Work: Provide guidance and support as your child transitions to college, vocational training, or employment. Help them explore career options, research educational programs, and develop job-seeking skills (e.g., resume writing, interview preparation).

Investigate available support services and accommodations in college or workplace settings, such as disability services, tutoring, counseling, and mentorship programs.

Encourage Independence and Responsibility: Encourage independence and responsibility by gradually increasing your child's autonomy in decision-making, problem-solving, and self-management. Provide opportunities for them to take on age-appropriate responsibilities and learn from their experiences.

Offer guidance and support as needed, but allow your child to take ownership of their choices and learn from both successes and setbacks.

Regular Check-Ins and Adjustments: Maintain regular check-ins with your child to discuss progress, challenges, and goals related to the transition to adolescence and adulthood. Be flexible and willing to adjust strategies and plans based on their evolving needs and preferences.

Encourage reflection and self-evaluation to promote self-awareness and growth throughout the transition process.

By implementing these strategies and fostering a supportive and empowering environment, parents can help their child with ADHD navigate the transition to adolescence and adulthood with confidence, resilience, and success. It's important to approach the transition as a collaborative effort, with a focus on building skills, fostering independence, and promoting overall well-being.

8.2 Building Independence and Life Skills

As people with ADHD enter adolescence and adulthood, they must develop their independence and life skills. The following are some methods to support the development of life skills and independence:

Clarify Your Expectations: Make sure everyone knows what is expected of them in terms of conduct, duties, and tasks. Divide up the work into doable chunks and provide clear directions on how to finish each one. Stress the significance of keeping your word and fulfilling deadlines.

Promote Making Decisions: Encourage your kid to take responsibility for their actions and make age-appropriate judgments. Provide direction and assistance when required, but let them bear the repercussions of their decisions and grow from their errors.

Give your kids the chance to develop their critical thinking and problem-solving abilities by talking about real-world situations and trying out various solutions together.

Teach Time Management and Organization: To assist your kid in keeping track of assignments, appointments, and deadlines, teach them organizing techniques like utilizing planners, calendars, to-do lists, and digital applications.

Establishing priorities, predicting the time needed for activities, and breaking down bigger projects into smaller, more manageable ones will all help your kid learn time management skills. To help them remain on task and efficiently manage their time, encourage them to set timers or alarms.

Encourage Self-Care Habits: Instill in your kid the value of self-care routines like eating a balanced diet, sleeping sufficiently, exercising on a regular basis, and leading a healthy lifestyle.

Encourage your kids to establish self-care routines that enhance their wellbeing and help them cope with stress, such as learning relaxation methods, going outside, or taking up a hobby they love.

Promote Financial Literacy: Instruct students on fundamental financial principles including saving, budgeting, and prudent spending. Assist your youngster in learning sound financial management techniques and goal-setting. Give your kids the chance to learn financial skills like setting up a savings account, keeping track of spending, and making wise purchases.

Encourage Advocacy and Communication Skills: Your kid should be encouraged to speak up for their needs and communicate clearly with others, including teachers, employers, and healthcare professionals. Teach children how to communicate assertively and encourage them to politely voice their opinions, worries, and preferences.

Talk to your kid about their rights, accommodations, and coping mechanisms for difficult circumstances relating to ADHD in order to support their development of self-advocacy skills.

Promote the development of independent living skills: Instruct students in independent living skills that are relevant to their daily lives, such as food shopping, cooking, cleaning, and washing. To help your kid develop competence and confidence, start including them in domestic activities and responsibilities at a young age.

Give your kids chances to practice life skills in authentic environments, such food planning and preparation, financial management, and using public transit.

Encourage self-reflection and goal-setting: Encourage your kid to make SMART (specific, measurable, realistic, relevant, and time-bound) objectives for themselves in both their academic and personal lives. Assist them in decomposing larger objectives into more manageable chunks.

Encourage a growth mentality by stressing the value of hard work, tenacity, and persistence in accomplishing objectives. Promote introspection and acknowledge advancements and successes along the road.

Demonstration of Self-reliance and accountability: Set a good example for others by acting responsibly and independently in everyday situations. Set an example of efficient problem-solving, planning, time-management, and self-care that your kids can follow.

Give your kids the chance to see and take part in making decisions, solving problems, and doing chores around the home so they may learn by doing.

Parents may assist their kid with ADHD acquire the independence and life skills necessary to succeed in adolescence and adulthood by putting these techniques into practice and offering continuing advice and support. Leading with autonomy, building resilience, and boosting self-esteem are essential components in equipping people with ADHD for future opportunities and challenges.

8.3   Exploring   Career   and Educational Opportunities

For those with ADHD, examining educational and employment options is a crucial part of making the move to adulthood. The following techniques may aid in successfully navigating this process:

Determine Your Interests and Strengths: Assist your kid in discovering their hobbies, interests, and abilities. Investigate the interests, pastimes, and academic fields in which they shine. When considering employment and educational possibilities, take into account their distinct abilities and interests.

Investigating Careers: Encourage your youngster to investigate other areas of interest and career alternatives. Doing research on various sectors, professions, and work positions might give students an idea of possible career routes.

To explore several jobs and get practical experience, take into consideration career evaluation tools, internships, volunteer opportunities, job shadowing, and informative interviews.

Routes for Education: Talk to your kid about the many possibilities and routes for their education, such as certificate programs, college, apprenticeships, and vocational training. Examine several majors, academic programs, and learning settings that fit their interests and professional objectives.

Take into account elements including your learning preferences, academic skills, desired job path, and the accommodations you'll need to succeed in school.

Getting Ready for College: Encourage your youngster to apply to and get admitted to colleges. Assist them in locating technical schools, colleges, and universities that provide courses related to their interests and aspirations for their careers.

Help with writing resumes, essays, recommendation letters, and college applications. To find out more about potential colleges, encourage your kid to visit college fairs, information sessions, and campus tours.

Trade Schooling and Apprenticeships: Examine the career technical education (CTE), apprenticeship, and vocational training options in your community. These courses provide practical experience and instruction in certain trades or sectors.

Make contact with neighborhood community colleges, skilled trades groups, and vocational schools to learn more about training programs and apprenticeships in industries including healthcare, construction, technology, and skilled crafts.

Skills for Job Readiness: Instill in your kid the fundamentals of professional communication, résumé writing, interview technique, and workplace decorum. Help them become more confident and prepared for employment interviews by having them role-play interview situations and offering feedback.

Assist your kid in acquiring real-world skills for the job, such flexibility, problem-solving, time management, organization, and cooperation. Give them the chance to get experience in the workplace via volunteer work, part-time employment, or internships.

Seek Support and Accommodations: Look into the supports and adjustments that are available for people with ADHD in the workplace and in educational settings. Together with disability services offices, businesses, and school counselors, find and implement adjustments that will help your kid succeed academically and at work.

Invoke the Americans with Disabilities Act (ADA) and other pertinent laws to protect your child's needs and rights. Assist them in acquiring the self-advocacy skills necessary to express their needs and look for suitable accommodations and assistance.

Examine Other Routes: Acknowledge that not every person with ADHD is a good match for the typical academic route. Investigate other choices including self-directed learning, trade schools, online learning, remote education, and entrepreneurship.

Encourage your kid to think about sectors and professions that encourage creativity, innovation, and specialized abilities, as well as non-traditional career routes.

Promote Growth and Lifelong Learning: Stress the value of ongoing professional and personal growth as well as lifetime learning. Throughout their professional path, encourage your kid to look for chances for skill improvement, certifications, and additional training.

Encourage resilience, flexibility, and an openness to taking on new challenges and growth chances to cultivate a growth mindset.

People with ADHD may find their hobbies, develop their abilities, and pursue rewarding careers and educational routes that complement their strengths and goals by investigating professional and educational options in a collaborative and supportive way. Fostering independence, promoting curiosity, and offering continuing support are essential components in assisting people with ADHD in making the transition to adulthood and establishing fulfilling lives and jobs.

8.4 Advocating for Continued Support and Understanding

It is critical to advocate for ongoing awareness and support for people with ADHD as they go through different phases of life. The following are some successful advocacy tactics:

Recognize Your Rights: Learn about the rights and protections provided to people with ADHD by laws including the Individuals with Disabilities Education Act (IDEA), Section 504 of the Rehabilitation Act, and the Americans with Disabilities Act (ADA). Recognize the adjustments and services for assistance that are offered in the workplace, community, and educational contexts.

Effective Communication: Share your child's needs, strengths, and ADHD-related difficulties with educators, employers, healthcare professionals, and other relevant parties in an honest and forceful manner. Take the initiative to start conversations with others about the adjustments, accommodations, and support techniques that may help your kid achieve.

Give information regarding evidence-based treatments for ADHD, its symptoms, and how it affects day-to-day functioning. To bolster your advocacy efforts, provide pertinent records, assessments, and advice from medical experts.

Work Together with Experts: Work together with educators, administrators, and specialists in special education to create and carry out Section 504 or individualized education plans (IEPs) that are tailored to your child's specific needs. Engage fully in progress evaluations, review meetings, and IEP meetings to make sure your child's educational requirements are being satisfied.

To get your kid the proper medical care, therapy, and support services for their ADHD, collaborate with doctors, therapists, and counselors. Encourage people to have access to behavioral therapy, medication management, evidence-based therapies, and social and emotional support when they need it.

Boost Your Self-Advocacy Ability: Help your kid learn how to speak out for themselves and to advocate for their own needs and rights. Teach children how to express their preferences, difficulties, and strengths so they may ask for help and accommodations when they need it.

Encourage your kid to stand out for themselves in a variety of situations, validate their experiences, and build resilience in order to help them develop a sense of self-awareness and self-confidence.

Keep Up to Date and Informed: Keep up with the most recent findings, innovations, and recommended procedures for the support, management, and treatment of ADHD. Attend conferences, seminars, and workshops to network with other ADHD-affected families and get knowledge from professionals.

Keep abreast of modifications to laws, rules, and policies that impact people with ADHD. Additionally, support programs and policies that advance equality, inclusion, and accessibility for people with neurodevelopmental disorders.

Create Support Systems: Make relationships with other community members who are parents, caregivers, or champions for ADHD and who have similar experiences and worries. Participate in online discussion boards, advocacy groups, and support groups for people with ADHD.

Seek direction, counsel, and support from colleagues who have faced comparable difficulties and who can provide perceptions and useful tactics for successful advocacy.

Record and Track Development: Maintain thorough records of your child's medical, behavioral, and academic history, along with exams, assessments, plans for treatment, and updates on their progress. Keep a record of all conversations, meetings, and encounters pertaining to speaking up for your child's needs.

Throughout time, keep an eye on your child's development and well-being, and be ready to modify tactics, modifications, and interventions as necessary to ensure their success and ongoing growth.

Encourage Comprehension and Awareness: Encourage more people in communities, businesses, and educational institutions to be aware of, accept, and understand ADHD. Inform others on the reality of having ADHD and dispel prejudice, stigma, and misunderstandings.

Encourage the development of a welcoming, compassionate, and supportive environment that values the contributions and abilities of people with ADHD and other neurodiverse illnesses.

You may contribute to the development of settings that are favorable to the success, wellbeing, and inclusion of people with ADHD by pushing for ongoing support and understanding. Your advocacy work is essential to ensure that people with ADHD have access to the tools, chances, and assistance they need to prosper and realize their full potential.